Fox at the Den

By Debbie Croft

Yin the Bun is at the den.

Mum went to get yams.

Big Fox can see Yin.

But he can not go
in the den.

Big Fox gets a wig,
rod and yam.

Yin can see Big Fox
has a wig.

Mum hops to the den.

Big Fox runs off.

Mum and Yin hug.

CHECKING FOR MEANING

1. What does Mum do at the start of the story? *(Literal)*

2. How does Big Fox try to trick Yin? *(Literal)*

3. Why doesn't Yin hug Big Fox? *(Inferential)*

EXTENDING VOCABULARY

yam	What sounds are in the word *yam*? If you take away the *y* and put an *r* at the start, what word can you make? What other name do we use for a yam?
fix	Look at the word *fix*. What sounds make up this word? Now find the word *fox* in the story. Which sound is different?
yum	What does this word mean? What other words do you know that mean the same? If you change the middle letter to an *a*, what is the new word?

MOVING BEYOND THE TEXT

1. Why is a den a safe place for a rabbit?

2. What do foxes usually eat?

3. How do foxes hunt and catch food?

4. How and where do yams grow?

SPEED SOUNDS

Xx	Yy	Zz				
Kk	Ll	Vv	Qq	Ww		
Dd	Jj	Oo	Gg	Uu		
Cc	Bb	Rr	Ee	Ff	Hh	Nn
Mm	Ss	Aa	Pp	Ii	Tt	

PRACTICE WORDS

yams

Yin

Fox

fix

yam

yum

Yes

Zip